U.S. Fire Administration/Technical Report Series

Special Report: Trends and Hazards in Firefighter Training

USFA-TR-100/May 2003

U.S. Fire Administration Major Fire Investigations Program

The U.S. Fire Administration develops reports on selected major fires throughout the country. The fires usually involve multiple deaths or a large loss of property. But the primary criterion for deciding to write a report is whether it will result in significant "lessons learned." In some cases these lessons bring to light new knowledge about fire--the effect of building construction or contents, human behavior in fire, etc. In other cases, the lessons are not new, but are serious enough to highlight once again because of another fire tragedy. In some cases, special reports are developed to discuss events, drills, or new technologies or tactics that are of interest to the fire service.

The reports are sent to fire magazines and are distributed at National and Regional fire meetings. The reports are available on request from USFA. Announcements of their availability are published widely in fire journals and newsletters.

This body of work provides detailed information on the nature of the fire problem for policymakers who must decide on allocations of resources between fire and other pressing problems, and within the fire service to improve codes and code enforcement, training, public fire education, building technology, and other related areas.

The Fire Administration, which has no regulatory authority, sends an experienced fire investigator into a community after a major incident only after having conferred with the local fire authorities to insure that USFA's assistance and presence would be supportive and would in no way interfere with any review of the incident they are themselves conducting. The intent is not to arrive during the event or even immediately after, but rather after the dust settles, so that a complete and objective review of all the important aspects of the incident can be made. Local authorities review USFA's report while it is in draft form. The USFA investigator or team is available to local authorities should they wish to request technical assistance for their own investigation.

For additional copies of this report write to the U.S. Fire Administration, 16825 South Seton Avenue, Emmitsburg, Maryland 21727 or via USFA Web page at http://www.usfa.dhs.gov

Special Report:
Trends and Hazards in Firefighter Training

Reported by: Adam Thiel
Jeff Stern
John Kimball
Nicole Hankin

This is Report 100 of the Major Fires Investigation Project conducted by Varley-Campbell and Associates, Inc./TriData Corporation under contract EMW-97-CO-0506 to the U.S. Fire Administration, Federal Emergency Management Agency, and is available from the USFA Web page at http://www.usfa.dhs.gov

Homeland Security

Department of Homeland Security
United States Fire Administration
National Fire Data Center

U.S. Fire Administration

Mission Statement

As an entity of the Department of Homeland Security, the mission of the USFA is to reduce life and economic losses due to fire and related emergencies, through leadership, advocacy, coordination, and support. We serve the Nation independently, in coordination with other Federal agencies, and in partnership with fire protection and emergency service communities. With a commitment to excellence, we provide public education, training, technology, and data initiatives.

ACKNOWLEDGMENTS

The United States Fire Administration greatly appreciates the cooperation received from the following people and organizations during the preparation of this report:

International Society of Fire Service Instructors

Assistant Chief Roger A. McGary, Montgomery County (MD) Division of Fire and Rescue Services

Maryland Fire and Rescue Institute

Mr. Steven T. Edwards, Director

Mr. Russell Strickland, Assistant Director— Field Programs

North Carolina Department of Insurance Fire and Rescue Services Division

Mr. Tim Bradley

The Maryland Council of Fire and Rescue Academies

National Fire Protection Association

In addition, the following individuals served as peer reviewers for this report, providing invaluable insight and expertise. We are grateful for their participation.

Mr. James Arnold
Program Manager, Public Sector
Fire Protection Training Division
Texas A & M University, Engineering Extension Service

Tim Rogers
Battalion Chief
Charlotte, NC Fire Department

Douglas Stutz, Ph.D
Director, School of Fire and Environmental Sciences
Metro-Dade Community College
Miami, FL

TABLE OF CONTENTS

INTRODUCTION

The range of services provided by America's fire service continues to expand. In many areas, the local fire department is responsible for mitigating hazardous materials incidents, performing technical rescues, and providing emergency medical services. The threat of terrorist incidents further increases the fire department's responsibility, as firefighters must be taught to recognize the signs of a chemical or biological attack and the proper response. This expansion of the fire service's responsibilities means that less time and energy are available to focus on basic fire suppression skills and scenarios. Also, some of the newer missions present their own, inherent training dangers.

In addition, the personal protective gear being worn by firefighters today is excellent; some say that it is even too protective. Firefighters now can advance deeper into structures and get closer to the seat of a fire than in years past because the turnout gear protects well against heat, but this can create problems. A longer exposure to fire will rapidly deplete a firefighter's energy and air supply; and the firefighter will have a greater distance to travel to an exit in an emergency situation. Furthermore, as firefighters progress farther into a structure, more time elapses, which means the fire is more developed, hotter, and often closer to flashover. Due to the increased use of synthetic and polycarbonate construction materials, fires are burning hotter and faster than in the past, resulting in a higher potential for building collapse and flashover. Collapse becomes more likely because of the increased damage from the fire.

Safe, effective, and realistic firefighter training is essential in preparing the fire service to achieve its mission of preserving life and property. The dilemma posed by conducting realistic fire training is that fires, even in a training setting, are inherently dangerous. Yet, the fire service needs realistic scenarios to fully experience the environment of a fire and how to combat it. Even without the presence of live fire, training on the physically challenging and labor-intensive tasks of hose handling, tool work, and ladder operations pose a high potential for injuries.

From 1987-2001 there has been a 31 percent decrease in the incidence of structure fires throughout the United States. As a result of the decline in fires, firefighters on the whole have less fireground experience than their predecessors had a generation ago. As many of the more experienced firefighters and officers retire, they are replaced by young officers with comparably less fire experience.

As today's firefighters' collective, direct experience in fighting fires continues to diminish, there is great concern in the fire service that the inability to recognize flashover and building collapse—and to react quickly enough to avoid being caught by these two potentially fatal conditions—will continue to result in injuries and fatalities to firefighters. Complicating this situation is that live fire training with Class A combustible materials (especially in acquired structures) is being replaced by temperature-controlled, fuel-fed fires in non-combustible structures. Departments are relying less on live fire training for myriad reasons, including among others, environmental, safety, and cost.

This report examines recent injurious and fatal incidents involving training to determine lessons that can be used to prevent future injuries and deaths. The emphasis in this report is on fire-related training, particularly live-fire evolutions. It is, however, important to note that training-related injuries can and do occur during a variety of types of training. Also included is a discussion of training standards and common hazards as well as a brief analysis of the available data on the number and cause of training-related injuries and deaths.

SUMMARY OF KEY ISSUES

Issue	Comments
Training injury data	Since 1987, reported training-related injuries have increased by nearly 21 percent. In 2001, almost 7,000 training-related injuries were reported, reinforcing the need to analyze trends in training-related injuries to determine how best to prevent future injuries and deaths.
Burn buildings versus acquired structures	Live fire training buildings and simulators have made fire training safer than in the past, but generally do not provide the same quality of realism as live fire training in acquired structures.
Controlled training techniques	Closely controlled and repetitive procedures that simulate "actual" fire conditions have led to fireground injuries in cases where inexperienced firefighters have not been able to select the most appropriate tactical procedure. Firefighters must be taught to recognize the early signs of flashover and building collapse so they can take appropriate action quickly.
Training standards and procedures	In cases reviewed by this report in which serious injuries resulted, procedures from either the NFPA 1403 Standard or the department's own established procedures were violated. Failure to follow well-established standards and procedures occurred in virtually every training injury reviewed during this study.
Need for improved health |and wellness programs	Firefighters continue to become injured or killed as a result of poor physical fitness. Improved health and wellness programs can reduce firefighters' risk for heart attack and stroke and better overall physical fitness can reduce the risk of other injuries (e.g., sprains/strains).
New types of training with their inherent risks	The need to expand training to include technical rescue, hazardous materials, and EMS, for example, has increased the types of training hazards to which firefighters can be exposed.
Instructor expertise	Today's fire service instructors are more qualified and well versed in instructional methodologies than in the past. However, they may not have the same level of fireground experience as previous instructors, due in part to the decline in the number of structure fires over the past two decades.
Less time available for training in basic evolutions	In order to meet the demands of expanding fire service roles, advanced and technical training evolutions have increased, thus reducing the amount of time available to perform basic training evolutions on such subjects as hose, ladder, and tool work.
New technologies contribute to safety	Modern, computerized burn buildings, fed by propane or natural gas, have many built-in safety features for conducting live fire training. Modern personal protective equipment, such as turnout gear and SCBA, provide greater escape time in dangerous conditions such as flashover. Simulation technology has increased the margin of safety in training.
Future trends	New technologies, such as virtual reality and other simulators, will inevitably become part of the training tools used by firefighters. These technologies can enhance, but not substitute for actual, live fire evolutions.

BACKGROUND

The purpose of this report is to identify key concerns regarding the hazards of firefighter training and to explore how the training hazards have changed. A goal of this report is to help fire departments reduce these hazards by offering suggestions based on the experiences of the study participants. Since behavior on the fireground is closely related to behavior on the training ground or drill field, it stands to reason that correcting safety-related issues during firefighter training should translate into fewer fireground injuries and deaths. A well-known fire department saying is: "train as you fight and fight as you train."

This report examines the state of safety in firefighter training as widely conducted in the United States. The results of this research are intended to help fire departments identify training hazards, improve the safety of trainees, and provide more effective and safe practical training. Although it is impossible to identify every training hazard, this report will analyze several of the most common hazards encountered during training evolutions. Some suggestions for addressing these hazards also are included.

The broad nature of this topic, combined with the limited amount of available data, necessitated that project staff solicit information from a variety of sources. To ensure broad input for the report, interviews were conducted with administrators, trainers, and other fire department personnel concerned with fire-rescue training. These interviews were informal, but structured as guided discussions.

Several meetings were conducted with local and state fire training officers to obtain information and develop a subjective sense of the key issues related to safe fire training. Project staff also conducted informal interviews with instructors and officers at several conferences, including the Fire Department Instructor's Conference in Indianapolis held in the spring of 1998. A wide array of literature on fire training was also reviewed using the National Fire Academy's Learning Resources Center.

TRAINING INCIDENTS

In the course of research for this study, a number of well-documented incidents were reviewed. Also, anecdotal information was provided by interviewees who related situations where training exercises resulted in minor injuries or very close calls. The following examples demonstrate the nature and extent of training hazards and their impact.

One firefighter killed, two injured in live fire training exercise

In September 2001, a firefighter died and two firefighters were injured while participating in a multi-agency, live-burn training evolution. Two of the firefighters were playing the role of firefighters in distress on the second floor. They became trapped when the training fire progressed up the stairwell, accelerated by a foam mattress, which had been ignited on the first floor. Two victims (including the deceased) were found in the upstairs bedroom where they had been positioned for the scenario; a third firefighter jumped to safety from a rear bedroom on the second floor.

The deceased had only been a volunteer for several weeks and had not received any formal fire suppression training before the live burn evolution. Following the incident, investigators found numerous violations of NFPA 1403, including the use of personnel as victims, the absence of training in the case of the firefighter who died, the lack of charged hoselines prior to ignition, and the placement of training fires near egress routes. In addition, the department's First Assistant Chief was convicted of criminally negligent homicide for his actions leading up to and during the incident.

Recruit killed during physical training

In July 2002, a recruit died while participating in physical training. His death occurred on the third day of recruit school; it was only the second day his class had participated in physical training. For their first physical training session the recruits ran approximately 2.78 miles. The next day, their physical training included a run of over 4 miles, a session of calisthenics, wind sprints, and jumping jacks. The heat index that morning ranged from 80 degrees Fahrenheit at 0700 when training began to 99 degrees Fahrenheit at 0825 when the recruit was en route to the hospital. He was pronounced dead an hour later with the cause of death listed as hyperthermia.

The department's Board of Inquiry found the following circumstances led to the recruit's death:

- The recruits had no opportunity or means to hydrate themselves during physical training.

- There was an unacceptable ratio of instructors to students; only one instructor was responsible for overseeing the recruits on the morning of the incident.

- The instructor leading the physical training session did not have a portable radio or cell phone to use in case of emergencies.

- There was a delay in activating an EMS response because the recruit's condition was not initially recognized as a true medical emergency.

Two firefighters injured during demonstration in improvised structure

At a department open house in 1996, two firefighters received minor burn injuries during a fire-fighting demonstration involving a mock-up of a house. The structure (12-1/2 feet by 7 feet by 7 foot), made of furniture crates, was designed to look like a house so that the fire department could simulate a fire attack for the public. The firefighters who entered the fully involved structure received first and second degree burns. The department's own review indicated that failure to provide senior level supervision and to comply with the 1992 edition of NFPA 1403 contributed to the outcome. Included in the findings were:

- There was no single officer in charge.

- No safety officer or rapid intervention crew was designated.

- Vertical ventilation was not conducted.

- The injured firefighters and the officer did not have sufficient experience for the structural firefighting demonstration.

- The firefighters had received initial training in a propane-fueled burn building. They had not, however, been taught how to attack a fire that was engulfing or blowing out of a door, as was the case in the demonstration.

- The improvised structure was totally inappropriate for any entry for training or demonstration purposes.

The department has since adopted NFPA 1403 Standard (1997 Edition) as its live fire training policy.

Three firefighters burned in improvised training structure during search and rescue

In late 1992, three firefighters were seriously burned while conducting training in a modified school bus that had been converted for use as a search and rescue simulator. The windows of the bus had been welded shut, no roof ventilation holes were cut, and the front door had accidentally jammed shut after the trainees and the instructor entered the bus. The operation had no incident command system, no safety officer, no back-up line, and no emergency medical standby.

The training evolution consisted of firefighters entering a burning, smoke-filled structure and completing search and rescue without a hoseline. No check was made of the firefighters' gear as they went into the former passenger area of the bus.

The fire had been allowed to pre-burn for 10 minutes. Conditions degenerated into flashover while the crew was inside. One firefighter was trapped inside after the disorganized exit by the others. He went into respiratory arrest as he was removed from the bus, and he was revived. That firefighter spent over two months in a critical care burn unit. Two others were less seriously burned, but required weeks of care in burn units.

One of the major lessons of this incident was the recognition of the inappropriate nature of such improvised structures (e.g., a modified school bus) for such a hazardous operation. The near-total lack of organization and safety procedures is also a major lesson from this unfortunate incident.

Chem-bio training leads to near fatal exposure to toxic products

In 1997, a member of a unit training to respond to a chemical incident was overcome by a nerve agent and exhibited signs and symptoms of central nervous system injury (seizures). This live-agent training evolution was designed to familiarize the student with the proper use of their protective equipment and clothing. Fellow students had to deliver doses of an antidote to stop the seizure.

Near miss when aerial ladder contacts high voltage electrical wires during training

In 1994, two firefighters narrowly escaped serious injury while conducting aerial training on the front ramp of their fire station. The firefighters were under the supervision of an experienced firefighter when he was called to the phone. The two firefighters, who were on the turntable of the ladder truck, decided to raise the ladder out of its bedded position while their colleague was away from the scene. Due to an incline at the front ramp of the station, the turntable free-rotated directly into high voltage power lines that ran in front of the firehouse, energizing the aerial ladder and burning a four foot hole through the asphalt under one of the ladder's jack plates. The two firefighters did not know how to engage the manual, turntable brake to prevent the ladder from turning. Firefighters inside the station calmed the firefighters until the power company could de-energize the wires. The firefighters were unhurt (the ladder truck sustained some damage and subsequently had to be returned to the manufacturer for repair).

Marine firefighting session injures instructor

In 1998, one firefighter was injured when the use of gasoline at a marine firefighting training session led to a vapor explosion. His hand was burned when he removed a glove to light the training fire. Marine firefighting is not addressed under NFPA 1403, but the individual survived with minor injuries, primarily because he was wearing full turnout gear and SCBA, which is required by NFPA 1403.

Apparatus accident injures firefighter, damages new engine

A firefighter was injured in 1998 when the engine in which he was riding rolled over during driver training. The incident occurred on the fire department's driver training course. The driver panicked while descending a hill, and stepped on the accelerator instead of the brake. He received minor injures; the engine, a newly delivered unit that had not yet been placed in service, was severely damaged

Recruit injured during power saw operations

A pair of experienced instructors was directing a group of recruits in the use of a gasoline- powered rescue saw on automobiles. One evolution involved cutting an auto door at the hinge assembly. After one such activity, one of the recruits told an officer that something hit his foot, but that he "was all right." Several exercises later, the recruit told the officer "his foot really hurt and he didn't feel well." The officer called for EMS support.

Examination revealed that one of the latch springs had apparently been propelled by the saw blade into the top of his foot. The spring hit beyond the area covered by the steel toe of the standard fire-fighter boot, penetrating the rubber boot and piercing the dorsalis pedis artery. The recruit suffered serious blood loss, was treated for shock, and was transported to a medical care facility. This incident emphasizes the need for scrutiny of all injuries, no matter how minor they may appear, and have EMS support available at all times during practical evolutions.

Firefighters injured in ad hoc training evolution

An engine company was participating in regularly scheduled training evolutions at their academy when an officer suggested a maneuver he had seen in a trade magazine. The evolution involved escape from flashover conditions utilizing a ground ladder at an extremely low angle placed below the sill of the "escape" window. Permission was granted and one of the firefighters attempted the maneuver, which required that he exit the window headfirst, and move down the ladder on all fours. The firefighter lost his balance and tumbled down the ladder, breaking a leg. While the initiative to try a new technique is highly commendable and should not be stifled, all training evolutions require careful consideration and verification that safeguards are in place.

Further, the head-first ladder escape (or ladder bail/slide) is considered the escape method of last resort and training on this technique should only occur in controlled situations.[1]

Deviation from established training procedures results in a near tragedy during a fire training exercise.

In this incident, fire academy staff applied drywall to two rooms of a structure that was acquired to conduct interior fire attack training. Per local environmental and departmental health regulations, the asbestos had been stripped from all walls and other enclosures.

The interior training staff, consisting of the safety officer and the igniter, started a fire outside the drywalled area for an "orientation" fire to practice limited interior attack. The fire rapidly progressed

---

[1] For more information, see the USFA Technical Report *Rapid Intervention Teams and How to Avoid Needing Them* at www.usfa.dhs.gov

to the attic and roof area, and the structure quickly became heavily involved. The interior crew had a properly connected safety hoseline, but the line was in the dry-walled area with the now-raging fire. The crew was cut off from the safety line as well as their primary means of escape, and they had to retreat out a bathroom window. This close call, caused by deviation from an established procedure, resulted in minor burns, but had the potential for disastrous results.

TRAINING CASUALTY DATA

The threshold at which fire departments report injuries (including training-related injuries) varies. Whether or not to report an injury is often based on the type and severity of an injury. For example, a burn injury is more likely to be reported than a minor strain that does not require either hospitalization or involve an insurance claim.

Various agencies and organizations collect and analyze the injury data that is reported. Some data on training-related injuries are available from the Occupational Safety and Health Administration (OSHA). Limited data are also available from the United States Fire Administration's National Fire Incident Reporting System (NFIRS) database. The National Fire Protection Association reports on injuries from its annual fire department survey.

Fatality data are more readily available than injury data, as the USFA and NFPA both track annual firefighter fatalities and publish annual reports on the topic. Further, the National Institute for Occupational Safety and Health (NIOSH) routinely investigates incidents involving firefighter fatalities. (NIOSH also investigates incidents involving firefighter injuries to a lesser degree.)

This section provides a brief overview of the available data on training-related injuries and fatalities. Anecdotal remarks, gathered during the interview process for this report, are also included. In the future, the fire service could benefit greatly from improving its tracking of firefighter injuries and targeting injury prevention efforts according to the information on injuries.

Training Injuries—From 1987 to 2001, an average of 6,700 training-related injuries was reported each year. As shown in Figure 1 Common Types of Training-Related Injuries Figure 1, the leading type of training-related injury is sprains/strains followed by wound/cut/bleeding/bruise. That these types of injuries are common during training is not surprising. Heart attack or stroke-related injuries are low—firefighters who suffer a heart attack or stroke during training are more likely to die than survive and then have long-term problems.

Figure 1. Common Types of Training—Injuries Related
(Based On Averages From 1987-2001)

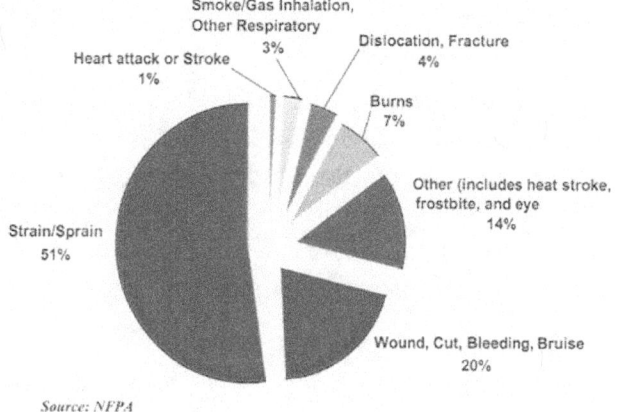

Source: NFPA

Figure 2 illustrates the rate of training-related firefighter injuries per 1,000 firefighters from 1987-2001. During this time period, the rate of reported training-related injuries increased by 15 percent. Over the same time period, the number of career and volunteer firefighters increased by only five percent.

The reasons for this upward trend in the rate of firefighter injuries are unclear. Given the increased training requirements for firefighters, it is likely that fire departments are devoting more time to training overall, thereby increasing the possibility of injury during such activities. Further, over the past 5-10 years, there has been an increased emphasis on health and wellness in the fire service, particularly on physical training and exercise. This presents the fire service with a double-edged sword—while physical fitness and exercise are critical to long-term health and wellness, as more firefighters become involved with physical fitness programs, the possibility of short-term injury increases.

Figure 2. Rate of Training-Related Injuries per 1,000 Firefighters (1987-2001)

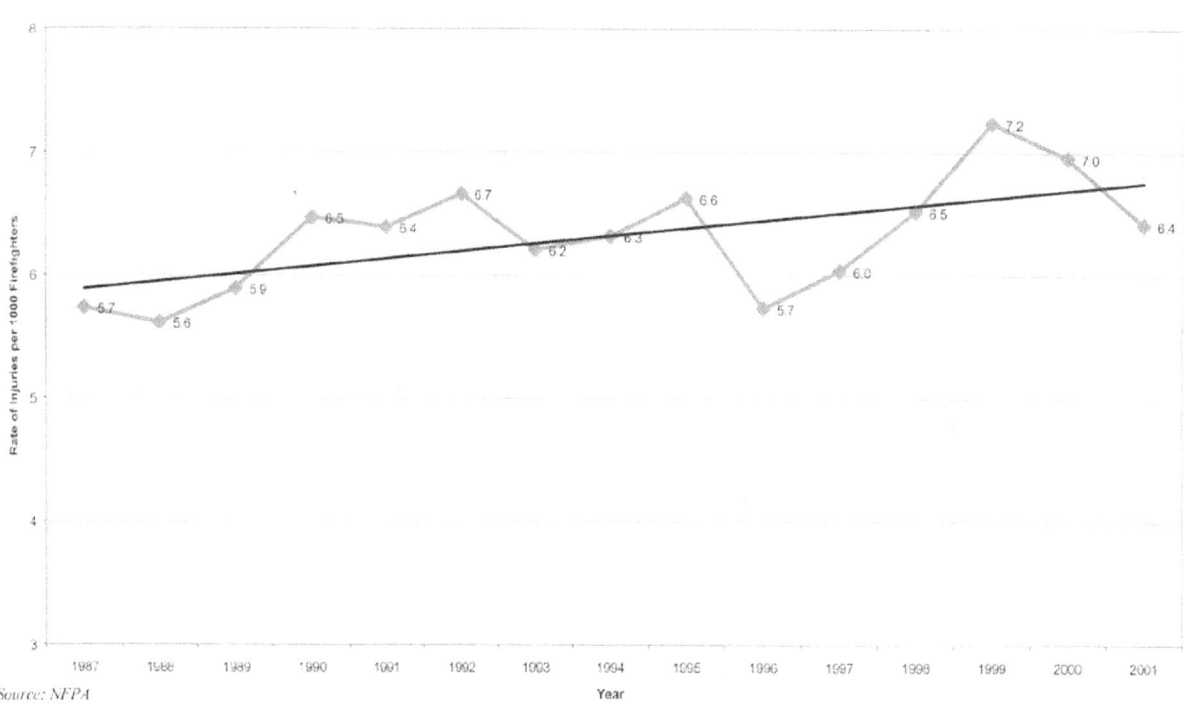

Source: NFPA

Accidents and Injuries During Driver Training—An area of significant concern raised by individuals who were interviewed was the number of accidents and injuries incurred during driver training. While reliable data are not available to determine the scope of this problem, its prevalence in anecdotal remarks suggests it may be an important issue. In fact, almost every interviewee could relate an accident or close call during driver training. Strict adherence to safety practices when training new drivers of emergency apparatus is underscored by these anecdotes.

Training Deaths—Since, 1978, training-related fatalities have trended upward (Figure 3). However, it is important to note that the number or training—related fatalities remains relatively small and as such, even small fluctuations can produce dramatic changes in the trend.

Figure 3. Training-Related Fatalities 1978-2001

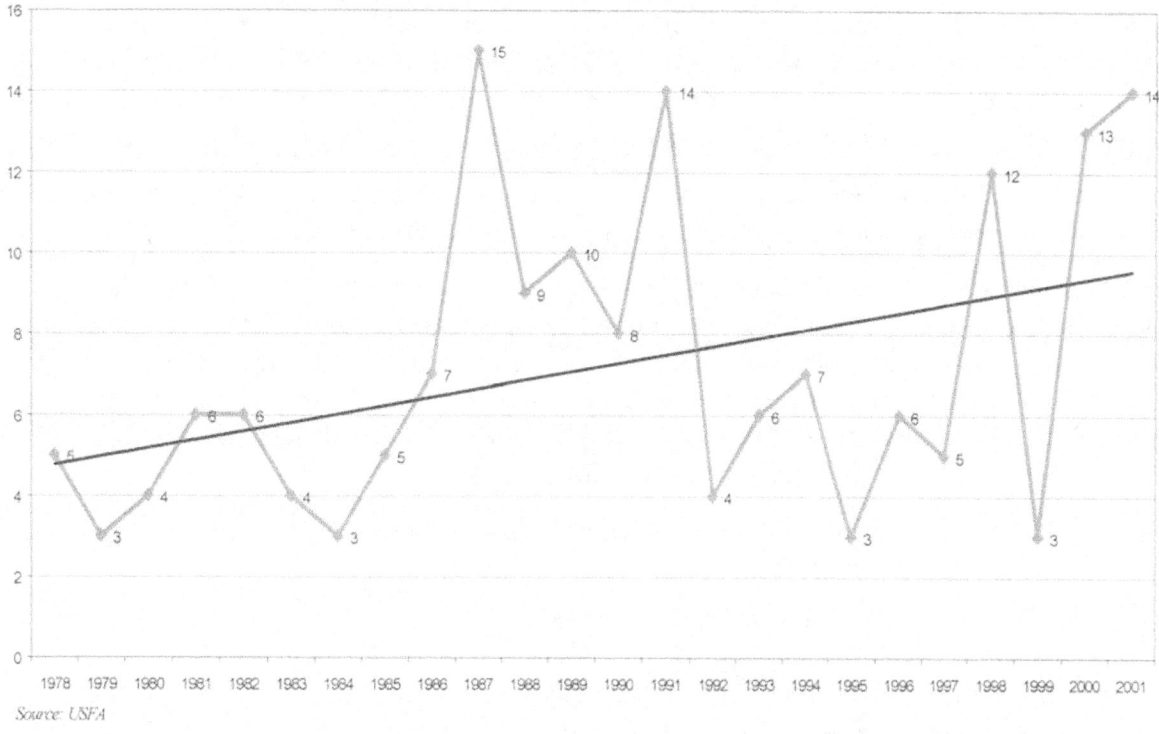

Source: USFA

Over time, the leading type of training activity that has resulted in fatalities has remained physical fitness training, followed by apparatus/equipment drills, and live-fire exercises. Heart attacks are the leading cause of death for training-related incidents, followed by trauma. Overall, the prevalence of heart attacks in firefighter fatality incidents is a source of much concern to the fire service. Increasingly, departments are offering health and wellness programs to their employees and members to help firefighters address modifiable risk factors for heart disease (such as obesity, diabetes, and hypertension). Any congenital heart or lung problems or pre-existing conditions should be reported by firefighters so that training supervisors can monitor their condition closely during physical fitness activities and physically stressful drills and exercises.

Fire Service Training Standards and Regulations

A variety of standards and regulations apply to fire service training programs. As will be discussed in this section, these include standards developed by the NFPA as well as local, state, and Federal regulations.

The NFPA

The NFPA standards are recommendations and guidelines developed by committees of chief officers, volunteer representatives, union officials, and industry representatives. They are not per se, legally binding, but whether or not NFPA standards have been adopted locally or not they have become the "standard of care" for the industry. When litigation is considered, lawyers often turn to the applicable standard of care in determining their course of action. It is up to decision-makers in political jurisdictions to determine levels of acceptable risk and the degree of liability exposure they will tolerate.

NFPA 1500, Standard on Fire Department Occupational Safety and Health Programs—NFPA 1500 requires fire departments to establish and maintain a training and education program to prevent occupational deaths, injuries, and illnesses. Further, departments must provide training and education for all department members commensurate with the duties and functions that they are expected to perform. Training must conform to the individual requirements for each fire department function (e.g, firefighter, driver/operator, fire officer, and fire instructor).

In addition, NFPA 1500 requires live fire evolutions to conform to NFPA 1403 (see below) and specifies that a qualified instructor must supervise all training exercises.

NFPA 1403, Standard on Live Fire Training—NFPA 1403 was developed after a training incident in 1982, which resulted in the deaths of two firefighters. Compliance with 1403 (in addition to improvements in personal protective equipment) has helped improve safety during live fire training. Our research indicated that since the implementations of this standard, sever burn injuries or major trauma during live fire training have occurred mostly when a department has deviated from the standard. Some of the major points of NFPA 1403 include:

- Fuels, such as pressure-treated wood, rubber, plastic, straw, and hay treated with pesticides or chemicals, are prohibited.

- Flammable or combustible fuels are prohibited.

- A safety officer should be designated.

- The maximum student to instructor ratio should be 5:1.

- One instructor should be assigned to the backup line, and to each designated sector assignment.

- EMS should be provided on-site.

- No personnel shall play the role of a victim in the fire building.

- Only one fire at a time is permitted in *acquired* structures.

- Pre-evolution briefings must familiarize all personnel with the layout of the structure and location of emergency exits.

NFPA 1001, Standard on Firefighter Professional Qualifications; NFPA 1002, Standard for Fire Apparatus Driver/ Operator Professional Qualifications; and NFPA 1021, Standard on Fire Officer Professional Qualifications—These three standards address the minimum training and knowledge required for personnel to operate at various levels of the fire service rank structure. They are designed to provide clear and concise job performance requirements that can be used to determine that an individual, when measured to the standard, possesses the skills and knowledge to perform a specific function.

NFPA 1041, Standard for Fire Service Instructor Professional Qualifications—NFPA 1041 identifies three distinct levels of responsibility for instructors. At Level I, the instructor must assemble necessary course equipment and supplies, review prepared instructional materials, and deliver instructional sessions based on the prepared materials. At Level II, an instructor is expected to be able to develop course materials independently and deliver those materials to students. Level III applies primarily to administrators and requires personnel to develop agency policy for training programs.

At all levels, NFPA 1041 requires instructors to be cognizant of the safety of their students to ensure that classroom and practical evolutions are conducted in a safe, controlled manner.

Local, State, and Federal Regulations

Local, state and Federal regulations also govern training. State and local governments as well as individual fire departments establish minimum training requirements for fire suppression personnel. Such requirements typically comply with NFPA standards, but not necessarily. The Federal government also plays a role in fire service training. For example, OSHA requires annual facemask fit tests for firefighters.

Environmental Protection Agency Standards—Local, State, and Federal environmental regulations have a direct impact on conducting live fire training evolutions. Such regulations often limit the type and amount of fuel allowed to be burned, and may require disposal of toxic products of combustion as hazardous waste. These restrictions limit the conduct of fire training, ranging from burning in acquired structures to flammable liquid firefighting. Individual, as well as departmental liability, including severe fines, may result from violating such regulations. Additionally, the safety of training participants and staff may be compromised if the proper controls are not executed.

Environmental regulations have led many departments either to adopt new, more environmentally "friendly" training methods, or, unfortunately, to disregard the regulations. Other areas of environmental concern that should be considered when conducting training include air pollution regulations and the presence of asbestos or other obvious contaminants.

OSHA Regulations—The Federal Occupational Safety and Health Administration (OSHA) has developed a variety of regulations that apply to the fire service under the Code of Federal Regulations (CFR). States that assert their own jurisdiction for the enforcement of occupational safety and health issues are required to meet or exceed the Federal OSHA requirements.

Specifically, 29CFR1910 addresses topics ranging from portable wood/metal ladders to the storage and handling of hazardous materials to automatic fire detection and sprinkler systems. One of the most critical OSHA regulations is covered under 29CFR1910.134, which focuses on respiratory protection. This regulation establishes guidelines for fit-testing SCBA facepieces as well as operational requirements for interior firefighting ("two-in/two-out").

COMMON HAZARDS IN TRAINING

There are a variety of potential hazards during firefighter training evolutions. While it would be impossible to identify every potential hazard, some of the most commonly encountered are detailed in this section, including recommendations for addressing these hazards.

Live Fire Training

Although generally considered an essential part of firefighter training, practical evolutions utilizing live fire or smoke pose a significant risk to both trainees and instructors. The potential for injury is very real during this type of training and prudent instructors take numerous precautions to ensure the safety of the participants. The majority of severe injuries over the last several years have involved incidents where NFPA 1403 was not adequately applied. Strict adherence to NFPA 1403 helps prevent serious injury or death during live fire training by ensuring that adequate safety measures are taken prior to beginning the exercise.

Further, the nature of live fire training has been steadily changing over the past decade. The use of acquired structures for training has declined, and the use of concrete or masonry burn buildings has become the norm. It is possible, and not unusual, for a recruit firefighter to completely progress and receive certification through the NFPA 1001 Firefighter Training program without ever experiencing any uncontrolled fire behavior outside a building specifically designed for fire department training.

Burn Buildings—Burn buildings are designed to contain the fire without damage, virtually eliminating the chances of serious structural collapse. The size of the fire can be controlled depending on the type and amount of fuel used. Other hazards associated with real structures, such as burning chemical laminates, paints, and sealants, are reduced.

One downside to using burn buildings is that they do not provide as great a degree of realism as acquired structures. Firefighters are often taught extinguishing methods in the classroom, such as aiming a hose stream at the ceiling, using a designated stream pattern, or moving to the base of the fire. In some jurisdictions, however, students are not allowed to employ these patterns because the high degree of heat from the steam produced may cause expensive damage to the burn building structures. Therefore, students do not perform the training attack and extinguishment in the same manner as would be required on the fireground. Such training practices have led to reports of firefighters using poor fire attack methods once they are deployed in the field.

An associated problem (especially in burn buildings that do not use alternative fuel sources) occurs when the student does not fully extinguish the training fire, so that the fire can be readily reignited for the next student. While this has not resulted in specific training injuries, it has been related to injuries and close calls on the fireground where new firefighters have failed to completely extinguish the seat of a fire or have failed to operate a hoseline for the necessary length of time. The experience of moving in on a fire once it has been knocked down, varying nozzle settings to overhaul hydraulically, continuing to apply water, and aggressively pulling walls and ceilings to overhaul the fire are all skills that cannot be practiced when training is conducted in burn buildings.

A third problem regarding burn buildings is that they fail to teach students to react to the diverse conditions encountered in real fireground operations. Actual firefighting in burn buildings often takes place in the same one or two hardened, high temperature burn rooms. Students often develop a repetitive way of approaching these fires, use the same extinguishing methods every time in a continued setting which conditions them to delay extinguishment. Furthermore, they routinely enter the fire room without flowing water, whereas in a real-world situation, firefighters must often make varied approaches to reach the seat of the fire, often operating hoselines as they move toward the fire location, and even attacking the fire from a protected position outside a doorway. Firefighters may use varied methods, such as direct, fog, or combination streams to extinguish fires, depending upon the stage of the fire, its location, ventilation status, and the building construction.

Fire Simulators—A parallel change to the widespread use of burn buildings is the increasing use of fire simulators that use clean-burning propane or natural gas instead of less environmentally friendly fuels such as wood pallets and excelsior fuel loads. These state-of-the-art simulators use computer systems, which monitor the rooms for dangerous conditions, allow customized fire behavior, and incorporate automatic shutdown procedures. They allow an operator to control the fire from a control station and to quickly extinguish the fire in an emergency.

During the interview process, participants debated which was more dangerous propane or natural gas. However, no injury statistics could be found suggesting one type of fuel over the other. Both systems, however, provided a greater margin of safety compared to traditional class A or B fuels because the fuel sources can be shut down immediately.

In several cases, training in simulators has led to learned behaviors, which have actually had an adverse impact on fireground safety and resulted in injuries. One criticism of fire simulators is that they fail to teach firefighters to react to the fire conditions, and do not address the importance of evaluating the type and construction of the building on fire, and effectively reading smoke conditions.

Interviewees related instances where inexperienced firefighters failed to fully extinguish fires from the habit of just knocking them down as in training fires. The use of straight streams is usually avoided in burn buildings because of the effects on the heat resistant surfaces, but many fires clearly indicate the use of solid streams. Many recruits have never used solid streams on class A fires until they reach the field. Recruits have been seriously burned from standing up to observe the heat levels. They do not have the tactical experience to discern the demarcation line of dangerous levels of high heat. Injuries have also occurred from new firefighters standing up in a panic situation and being seriously burned. They have not encountered similar high heat conditions in a training situation and may not recognize the critical heat situations. The limited field experience levels of many fire instructors and fire officers, as is discussed elsewhere in this report, compound this hazard.

Acquired Structures—The use of an acquired or donated structure for live fire training generally offers the most realistic setting in which to train firefighters in fire suppression methods and operations. The simulation element in this type of training is minimal, as once the fire has been started, it more reasonably approximates the "real thing" compared to a gas-fed simulator. The NFPA 1403 Standard (1997 Edition) for live fire training covers the procedures that must be in place for live fire training in acquired structures. Proper application of these procedures has reduced the frequency and severity of injuries during fire training in acquired structures.

Improvised Structures—Improvised structures include mock-ups of structures and structural components, which are used for training or demonstration purposes. Some of these structures have increased the ability to safely train for certain fireground tactics. Roof simulators, for example, allow firefighters to conduct ventilation training on varied surfaces and at various degrees of pitch. These roof simulators are built to actual code and construction standards with cut-outs and replaceable panels so as to simulate actual roof conditions. When mock-up structures are improvised using low-grade materials, training injuries have occurred.

Flashover Simulators—Some fire departments have utilized the flashover simulator devices originally developed in Europe to give firefighters first-hand experience in observing flashover conditions. The training allows firefighters to watch how fire conditions build towards flashover and emphasizes how flashover can be delayed or prevented with proper application of hose streams. These simulators are credited with providing firefighters survival skills and tactics when they are caught in impending flashover conditions.

No serious injuries have been reported from the use of these flashover simulators, although many firefighters received minor steam burns due to damp gear from sweat after multiple training evolutions.

Future Technology—New technology is making its way into firefighter training. Simulators are now available for emergency apparatus operator training. Similar to aircraft flight simulator technology, the drivers are placed in a mock-up of an engine or vehicle cab, and computer screens simulate driving in various conditions and with numerous hazards such as other vehicles and pedestrians. This technology has the potential to increase the type and diversity of training scenarios available to firefighters while eliminating the risks of real accidents and injuries while conducting live training. However, the mental skills practiced in virtual reality simulators still have to be transitioned into operational experience. These technologies can greatly enhance the qualities of firefighter training, but cannot replicate the reality of driving an engine to an emergency or advancing a charged hoseline.

Other Types of Firefighter Training

The expansion of fire department services has increased the types of training hazards to which firefighters are exposed. These growing services include structural collapse training, trench rescue training, confined space rescue training, rope rescue training, dive rescue, surf rescue, swift water rescue, Hazmat, and counter-terrorism (chemical, biological, and nuclear) training. In some skills, such as confined space or trench rescue, NFPA and OSHA standards currently offer appropriate safeguards.

Training in these disciplines often requires training in the dangerous environment. While departments can conduct confined-space rescue training in safely designed simulators, a swift water rescue course must at some point place students in moving current, just as a fire trainee should eventually face live training fires.

One key difference between the Hazmat and technical rescue disciplines and fire training is that the technical disciplines often integrate a thorough risk assessment process which intentionally delays the actions of emergency responders until an action plan can be developed and appropriate resources are in place. Fire training, on the other hand, integrates a more rapid risk analysis and decisionmaking process which, while necessary on many emergency incidents, can lead to injuries in training. Training students in the rescue environment demands strong supervision, experienced instructors, a small student to instructor ratio, and in-place safety teams and procedures.

Physical Stress

Firefighting is, without question, a highly physical and demanding activity. The intensity and prolonged duration of firefighter training evolutions place substantial physical stress on trainees and instructors. Injuries that commonly occur during training evolutions involve knees, lower back, strains, and sprains. The best means for preventing these potential injuries is by promoting physical fitness and proper lifting techniques. Although it is impossible to completely prevent these types of injuries, increased fitness and conditioning helps to reduce the incidence of injury and enable firefighters to cope with the intense physical demands of practical training and tactical operations. Simple techniques, such as warm-up exercises to prevent muscle injuries, although not routinely employed, should be done prior to any training.

It is also important to rotate training crews and instructors during training to provide adequate time for rehabilitation. The risk of injury increases during later stages of live fire training if multiple scenarios are used in the same training session and fatigue becomes a risk factor.

Unsafe Practices

The discipline and supervision applied during training can rarely be matched in actual firefighting operations. In many ways, training can and should constitute one of the safest aspects of a firefighter's job. However, training is sometimes compromised by complacency or by the diminished sense of danger suggested in a controlled training environment.

Sometimes students and instructors alike take shortcuts or fail to observe safe/required practices. Study participants noted the following examples: jumping off apparatus, riding on the tailboard, and not fastening seat belts. Horseplay among trainees was also cited as a unit discipline problem. Although camaraderie is an important part of the training experience, horseplay may take attention off the task at hand and contribute to injuries.

Improper Use of Personal Protective Equipment—Although the increased efficiency of turnout gear has reduced the number of firefighter burn injuries, preventable injuries still occur with unnecessary frequency during practical evolutions. Some of these injuries can be attributed to the improper use of PPE including missing gloves, unbuttoned coats, unfastened collars, and unbuckled helmet chinstraps.

Respiratory injuries continue, despite the almost universal use of SCBA. Some of these injuries are attributable to SCBA that are incorrectly worn, improperly donned/doffed, not thoroughly checked prior to use, or not properly maintained.

Use of Accelerants—The 1997 edition of NFPA 1403 continues to advocate that accelerants not be used at live fire training. Several non-compliant training evolutions have resulted in serious injuries and deaths when accelerants were used to fuel training fires.

Attitude and The "Training Academy Way"—One of the cornerstones of fire service training is to impart the correct attitude towards firefighting from instructor to student. Failure to pass on the appropriate attitudes and force unit discipline in fire training can have a lasting effect on students. One problem consistently voiced by experienced fire service personnel is the attitude that there is a "training academy way" of doing things, and the "real" way of doing things (outside of training). The "training academy way" should be synonymous with the "right way."

Background Knowledge, Skills, and Abilities

As the fire service has grown to accommodate personnel from a more diverse background, the knowledge base among fire students has also changed. Twenty or thirty years ago, many firefighters possessed trade skills related to equipment and construction. Fire training could begin with certain assumptions as to the student's mechanical aptitude and ability to use basic hand tools. Some students today, however, may not know how to operate basic tools and machinery, or have any experience driving a large truck or operating manual transmissions. With widely divergent backgrounds, some students require fundamental training in the simple mechanical skills necessary for some basic firefighting operations.

When conducting field-training evolutions, especially those involving live firefighting, instructors may assume that trainees have the requisite knowledge and skills to perform ancillary functions involving ventilation, ground ladders, or ropes and knots. However, students may not have the necessary skills to perform unfamiliar functions. Instructors should identify such students in advance, and ensure that they are not called on to perform a skill for which they have not been adequately trained.

Instructor and Officer Fire-Combat Experience

The decrease in the incidence of structural fires, coupled with improvements in building construction and detection/suppression systems, has led to a shortage of instructors with extensive experience under actual fire conditions. As experienced instructors retire, especially those in career fire departments serving urban areas, they are being replaced with younger, less seasoned instructors. New instructors are often well educated and have usually achieved instructor certifications through organizations that meet or exceed NFPA standards for teaching and training. However, many of these instructors do not have the same level of fireground experience as more seasoned fire instructors. While well-trained and competent leaders, they may not have the fire combat experience of many of their predecessors that can help them to quickly recognize dangerously changing fire conditions. Limited experience makes it even more imperative that firefighting instruction adheres strictly to policies and standards established by the NFPA and local jurisdictions.

Environmental Hazards

Two environmental issues are prevalent with live fire training: first, environmental damage as a result of the training; and second, environmental hazards, which pose a danger to firefighters participating in drills.

Environmental Damage—Live fire training can result in damage to the environment through repeated release of products of combustion and run-off water from fire suppression operations. The smoke effects are localized and usually short term, while run-off has the potential to cause greater long-term damage to the local environment. Training personnel should guard against the potential for run-off damage to local streams, drinking water, and wildlife. Foam training is especially difficult because many class B foams should be cleaned up as hazardous waste. To address this, some departments have switched to using biodegradable class A foams or computer simulators for foam training.

Health Considerations—Personnel must be aware that the products of live fire training can also pose hazards to their long-term health and welfare. Because training often takes place in repeated evolutions over several hours, personnel are exposed to inhalation and absorption of products of combustion during that time. Personnel should be monitored continually for the effects of exposure during this time period. If training is conducted in accordance with NFPA 1403 standards, burning materials will consist of less hazardous class A products. But these still give off combustion products, such as carbon monoxide, which can build up in the bloodstream over several hours.

Some departments deviate from NFPA 1403, and use accelerants such as diesel fuel, which release toxic and carcinogenic chemicals. Other departments use donated materials, which may contain unknown chemical hazards or possess dangerous, combustible properties under fire conditions. The impact of prolonged exposure to such products is an exposure surveillance of special concern to training instructors, who may be exposed to these products on a regular and prolonged basis throughout their training careers. The long-term effects of this kind of exposure between training staff personnel and non-training personnel over the course of their lifetimes could benefit from an epidemiological study.

LESSONS LEARNED

Realistic firefighter training is essential for ensuring safe operations at true emergencies. Realistic training remains inherently hazardous, though policies and safety procedures have provided for a much greater degree of safety over the past twenty years. Because fire suppression operations are also inherently dangerous, the fire service should train firefighters in as close to actual conditions as possible, while protecting them in the process. The challenge for firefighters to push themselves to the boundaries of their capabilities is necessary for long-term firefighter survival. The following lessons should be considered as part of that delicate balance:

1. **Failure to follow established guidelines in training can lead to tragic outcomes.**

   Many of the injuries and fatalities over the past decade have been the result of failure to follow currently accepted procedures and standards.

2. **Fire service instructors should ensure that training standards and procedures be followed closely, especially when challenging tasks are assigned to recruits.**

   To prevent injuries, instructors must know their material well, maintain a high ratio of instructors to students and be vigilant about ensuring strict adherence to safety procedures. Instructors should familiarize themselves with the backgrounds and experience of their students, and care should be taken to avoid situations for which the students are not yet prepared.

3. **Burn buildings and other training technologies cannot substitute for the experience gained in "real" structure fires and live fire evolutions.**

   Since fire behavior and fire attack methods can vary between a burn building and a "real" structure, firefighters need to practice in both. Important skills, such as overhaul, cannot be easily replicated in burn buildings. It is increasingly important that firefighters receive training in fire behavior and extinguishment methods for different types of building construction.

4. **Modern SCBA and protective ensembles provide increased protection levels that require greater training and acquired skills. The recognition of life-threatening fire conditions may be less obvious as a result of the improved protective clothing and equipment.**

   One reported concern is that firefighters are now so fully encapsulated that they cannot feel the initial danger signs of rapid heat build-up. They are more likely to "go too deep" into a fire building, past the point when they can safely exit, thus negating the advantages provided by the gear. This concern has existed for more than a decade, and will likely continue. It underlines the importance of training firefighters to recognize the visual and physical clues to impending danger, such as reading changing smoke conditions and anticipating fire behavior in different types of building construction.

5. **Another concern is the number of firefighter fatalities related to physical condition. Cardiovascular failure continues to kill and disable firefighters while they are involved in training.**

Field experience with heart/cardiovascular-related events mirrors the record of training deaths due to heart attack and stroke. To reduce the amount of such fatalities, departments should consider stronger physical screening programs and long-term health and wellness programs. During training, a firefighter's physical stress-level should be monitored continuously, Adoption of, and compliance with, physical fitness standards should be closely monitored, and vigorously enforced and EMS should be readily available.

CONCLUSION

The fire service is faced with a challenge. Improvements in public fire education, prevention, detection, and building construction have resulted in fewer fires and reduced the amount of damage, both in terms of lives and dollars, inflicted by fire. At the same time, however, this trend has reduced the amount of on-the-job training experience available to firefighters and officers.

Training remains the key in developing safe and successful emergency responders. New technologies, which have increased the ability to push trainees to the "edge of the envelope," come with their own inherent flaws, as seen in several examples presented in this report. The adoption of training standards, implementation of and adherence to safety procedures, and proper supervision are the keys to preventing training injuries.

The need for safe firefighter training must be balanced with sufficient challenge to prepare firefighters for the unpredictable nature of the fireground. Training must not be so controlled as to give firefighters a false sense of security, nor can it disregard established safety procedures for the sake of increased realism. To maintain an effective cadre of firefighters and officers, the fire service must find new and dynamic ways to train personnel to act in a safe, decisive manner that best supports the fire service's mission to protect lives, property, and the environment.

Montgomery County (MD) Fire and Rescue Services

Live Fire Training Safety Documentation for NFPA 1403

(1992 Edition)

(used with permission)

MONTGOMERY COUNTY

DEPARTMENT OF FIRE & RESCUE SERVICE

LIVE FIRE TRAINING REQUEST DOCUMENTATION

Contact the DFRS Safety Office for guidance and assistance in completing
This document
May 1995

DEPARTMENT OF FIRE AND RESCUE SERVICES
MONTGOMERY COUNTY, MARYLAND

Field Support Services / Safety Office

Date: _____

To: _____

From: A.C. Roger A. McGary, Chief
Field Support Services/Safety

Subject: Live Fire Training Requirements

From time to time various Corporations or the Department are able to use acquired structures for live fire training. In many cases these structures present significant hazards to potential participants. Making the structure safe may require removal of asbestos shingles and stored fuel, installation of handrails and flooring, etc.

Because of the hazards associated with live fire training, a thorough inspection of the property must be made before any Department of Fire and Rescue Services employee participates. ONLY after an inspection, or reinspection by the DFRS Safety officer (or deputy safety officer), in which the property is found safe, will a permit to burn be issued.

Upon return of this document with the first two parts of Section 1 completed (Department request and owner information) and including the required attachments, an inspection of the property shall be scheduled. The initial inspection will follow the check list found in Section 1 under Building Inspection Form. Appropriate repairs and alterations will be required for each deficiency noted. A final inspection will be required when these changes have been completed. The inspection is done in accordance with the guidelines found in the National Fire Protection Association Standard 1403 *("Live Fire Training Evolutions in Structures," 1992 edition).*

FIELD SUPPORT SERVICES/SAFETY OFFICE

REQUEST FOR LIVE FIRE TRAINING

S U M M A R Y   C H E C K L I S T:

Prior to an inspection being initiated by a Department Safety Officer, the following information must be attached:

_____   A completed property owner checklist, with appropriate attachments
            (see pages 5 & 6).

_____   A water supply checklist (see pages 14 & 15).

_____   A lesson plan and scenario for each activity period where burning will occur
            (see page 17).

_____   A floor plan, and a pre-burn plan that will be provided to each participant at a pre-burn
            briefing (see page 19).

_____   A list of instructors and their assignments (see pages 21-26)

_____   A list of participants (see page 28)

_____   A plot plan showing distances to exposures, locations of hydrants, staging areas,
            alternate water supply, etc. (see page 18)

_____   Document unusual conditions, such as exposures and access problems
            (see page 18).

DEPARTMENT OF FIRE AND RESCUE SERVICES
MONTGOMERY COUNTY, MARYLAND

REQUEST FOR LIVE FIRE TRAINING

SECTION I

> Department Request

> Owner Information

> Inspection

> Re-inspection

FIELD SUPPORT SERVICES/SAFETY OFFICE

REQUEST FOR LIVE FIRE TRAINING

Fire Department Requesting Inspection:_____

Officer Requesting Inspection:_____

Contact Person for Inspection:_____

Address of property to be burned:_____

_____

Owner and agent of property:

*Name:*_____

Address:_____

*Phone/Pager:*_____

Fax (*or other*):_____

FIELD SUPPORT SERVICES/SAFETY OFFICE

REQUEST FOR LIVE FIRE TRAINING

P R O P E R T Y   O W N E R   C H E C K L I S T:

____ Attach a Montgomery County Department of Fire and Rescue Services *Permission to Burn Form (see page 6).*

____ Attach a photocopy of the deed to the property with appropriate documentation that the property is free and clear.

____ Provide a copy of a cancellation of insurance.

____ Provide a copy of a raising permit and a burning permit from Montgomery County Department of Environmental Protection.

____ Following completion of training who will be responsible for the leveling of all chimneys, filling in of the foundation and any other work that will insure the site is safe? Identify that person and have the appropriate signatures as noted below:

Responsible for site clean up:

Name:_____

Signature of authorized party: _____

Signed:_____
Fire Department Officer

FIELD SUPPORT SERVICES/SAFETY OFFICE

REQUEST FOR LIVE FIRE TRAINING

PERMISSION TO BURN

We, _____,

the undersigned, give the Montgomery County Department of Fire and Rescue Services and its
agents permission to burn the property we own, located at:

_____

   We will not hold the Montgomery County Department of Fire and Rescue Services,
Montgomery County Government, or its agents, responsible for any damage to our property, or
any other manner, before, during or after burning.

   We further understand that the Montgomery County Department of Fire and Rescue Services,
nor any of its agents, make any guarantees as to the condition of the structure after the burning is
over.

   All insurance that we have on this property has been cancelled, and no claims for insurance
will be made by anyone on said property. This property may be burned at the convenience of the
Montgomery County Department of Fire and Rescue Services, or any of its agents, within the
next _____ days.

Signed: _____
               Owner #1   Owner #2

Date Signed: _____

Signed: _____
               Fire Department Officer

Signed: _____
               Witness

BUILDING INSPECTION FORM

Initial/Follow-up/Final Inspection *(circle one)*

RESULTS / CONDITION OF AREA INSPECTED:	LIST SPECIFIC AREA INSPECTED BELOW:
OK? If so, check here:	Building inspected to determine structural integrity
Problems / Concerns / Comments:	
OK? If so, check here:	All utilities disconnected from acquired building
Problems / Concerns / Comments:	
OK? If so, check here:	Highly combustible interior wall and ceiling coverings
Problems / Concerns / Comments:	
OK? If so, check here:	Holes in walls and ceilings patched
Problems / Concerns / Comments:	
OK? If so, check here:	Materials of exceptional weight removed from above
Problems / Concerns / Comments:	training area (or area sealed from activity)
OK? If so, check here:	Ventilation openings of adequate size precut for each roof
Problems / Concerns / Comments:	area
OK? If so, check here:	Windows checked and operated, openings closed
Problems / Concerns / Comments:	
OK? If so, check here:	Doors checked and operated, opened or closed as needed
Problems / Concerns / Comments:	(but never nailed or barricaded closed)
OK? If so, check here:	Building components checked and operated
Problems / Concerns / Comments:	
OK? If so, check here:	Roof Scuttles
Problems / Concerns / Comments:	
OK? If so, check here:	Automatic ventilators
Problems / Concerns / Comments:	

BUILDING INSPECTION FORM

RESULTS / CONDITION OF AREA INSPECTED:	LIST SPECIFIC AREA INSPECTED BELOW:
OK? If so, check here:	Building components checked and operated: Sprinklers
Problems / Concerns / Comments:	
OK? If so, check here:	Building components checked and operated: Standpipes
Problems / Concerns / Comments:	
OK? If so, check here:	Stairways made safe with railing in place
Problems / Concerns / Comments:	
OK? If so, check here:	Chimney checked for stability (do not weaken or undercut
Problems / Concerns / Comments:	**chimney)**
OK? If so, check here:	Fuel tanks and closed vessels removed or adequately
Problems / Concerns / Comments:	**sealed**
OK? If so, check here:	Unnecessary inside and outside debris removed
Problems / Concerns / Comments:	
OK? If so, check here:	Porches and outside steps made safe
Problems / Concerns / Comments:	
OK? If so, check here:	Cisterns, wells, cesspools or other ground openings filled
Problems / Concerns / Comments:	
OK? If so, check here:	Hazards from toxic weeds, hives, and vermin eliminated
Problems / Concerns / Comments:	
OK? If so, check here:	Hazardous trees, brush and surrounding vegetation
Problems / Concerns / Comments:	
OK? If so, check here:	Exposures, such as buildings, trees, and utilities, removed
Problems / Concerns / Comments:	**or protected**
OK? If so, check here:	All extraordinary exterior and interior hazards remedied
Problems / Concerns / Comments:	

BUILDING INSPECTION FORM

Problems found and corrective action necessary:

_____
_____
_____
_____
_____
_____
_____
_____
_____
_____
_____
_____
_____
_____
_____
_____
_____
_____

Date Inspected Rank & Signature

Page 3 of 3

FIELD SUPPORT SERVICES/SAFETY OFFICE

REQUEST FOR LIVE FIRE TRAINING

PARTICIPANTS:

The following departments and the approximate number of people per department will participate:

Department of Fire and Rescue Services Personnel_____Total:_____

Fire Department:_____Total:_____

Fire Department:_____Total:_____

Fire Department:_____Total:_____

Fire Department:_____Total:_____

Fire Department:_____Total:_____

Fire Department:_____Total:_____

DEPARTMENT OF FIRE AND RESCUE SERVICES
MONTGOMERY COUNTY, MARYLAND

REQUEST FOR LIVE FIRE TRAINING

SECTION II

Training Ground Operations:

❯ Command Structure

❯ Instructor Details

❯ Training Scenarios

❯ Floor Plans

❯ Water Supply

FIELD SUPPORT SERVICES/SAFETY OFFICE

REQUEST FOR LIVE FIRE TRAINING

COMMAND STRUCTURE:

Incident Commander (Instructor in Charge):_____

Safety Officer:_____

PIO:_____

OPERATIONS   LOGISTICS   PLANNING   ADMINISTRATION/FINANCE

_____FIRE Sector

_____EMS Sector

_____STAGING

_____HAZMAT Sector

FIELD SUPPORT SERVICES/SAFETY OFFICE

REQUEST FOR LIVE FIRE TRAINING

LIVE FIRE TRAINING CHECKLIST:

INSTRUCTORS:

_____   Ratio: One instructor to five students.

_____   Assure that all protective clothing and equipment is used.

_____   Use Fire and Rescue Commission Policy and Procedure number 26-04. (Unit and Personnel Accountability).

_____   Assign an **Accountability** and **Entry Control** officer.

PROTECTIVE CLOTHING/EQUIPMENT:

_____   Ensure that self-contained breathing apparatus is used.

_____   Provide for sufficient spare cylinders for the self-contained breathing apparatus.

_____   Ensure that coats, bunker pants, boots, helmets, gloves, hoods, and pass devices, meeting Montgomery County standards, are used.

FUEL MATERIALS:

_____   Use NO unidentified materials.

_____   Only Class A materials (such as excelsior) can be used for initial ignition.

FIELD SUPPORT SERVICES/SAFETY OFFICE

REQUEST FOR LIVE FIRE TRAINING

LIVE FIRE TRAINING CHECKLIST (p.2)

WATER SUPPLY:

_____   Using the NFA Fire Flow Formula (length x width '/. 3 = gallons per minute per involved floor) identify here and on the water supply check-list the required fire flow for the training structure. *(NOTE: YOU SHOULD CALCULATE FOR A TOTALLY INVOLVED FLOOR, VS. A PERCENTAGE. THIS WILL PROVIDE AN ACCEPTABLE SAFETY FACTOR.*

_____   Identify here fire flow requirements:

_____   Fire flow required for training structure: _____GPM.

_____   Fire flow required for exposures: _____GPM.
         NOTE: USING THE NFA FORMULA - YOU REQUIRE 25% OF
         THE TOTAL FIRE FLOW FOR EACH EXPOSURE.

_____   Subtotal fire flow required: _____GPM.

_____   50% of total for unforeseen situations: _____GPM.

_____   Total all fire flow required: _____GPM.

_____   Fire flow capability of system: _____GPM.

Identify the hydrant locations, (also size of main and flow capacity, if known)

LOCATION: MAIN SIZE: FLOW:

_____   _____   _____
_____   _____   _____
_____   _____   _____
_____   _____   _____
_____   _____   _____

FIELD SUPPORT SERVICES/SAFETY OFFICE

REQUEST FOR LIVE FIRE TRAINING

LIVE FIRE TRAINING CHECKLIST (p.3)

WATER SUPPLY CHECKLIST (*Continued*):

Identify the location of the backup water supply sources:

_____

_____

_____

Identify the engine companies to be used for fire attack, and their locations (also place on plot plan):

_____

_____

_____

Identify the engine/tanker being used for the backup supplies (and show on plot plan):

_____

_____

_____

The water supply system must be capable of delivering over 100% of the total fire flow requirement for the structural building and exposures, plus an additional 50% of this requirement for other unforeseen situations.

Separate sources shall be utilized for attack and backup lines (two sources are required to preclude the loss of both the attack and backup water supply sources at the same time).

FIELD SUPPORT SERVICES/SAFETY OFFICE

REQUEST FOR LIVE FIRE TRAINING

LIVE FIRE TRAINING CHECKLIST (p.4)

INSTRUCTORS AND ASSIGNMENTS:

Instructors: Assignments:

_____   _____

_____   _____

_____   _____

_____   _____

_____   _____

_____   _____

SAFETY ASSIGNMENTS:

Safety Officer(s) assigned: _____

_____

Entry Control Officer:_____

Accountability Officer:_____

FIELD SUPPORT SERVICES/SAFETY OFFICE

REQUEST FOR LIVE FIRE TRAINING

PLANNED TRAINING SCENARIOS:

Identify the specifics of each planned training scenario.

Scenario 1:

_____

_____

_____

_____

_____

_____

Scenario 2:

_____

_____

_____

_____

_____

_____

Etc.

FIELD SUPPORT SERVICES/SAFETY OFFICE

REQUEST FOR LIVE FIRE TRAINING

PLOT PLAN

Provide a plot plan of the site to include:

> ❭ Exposures

> ❭ Roads

> ❭ Water supply

> ❭ Fire attack access

> ❭ Emergency escape

> ❭ Command Post

> ❭ Staging

> ❭ Any other planned assignments

FIELD SUPPORT SERVICES/SAFETY OFFICE

REQUEST FOR LIVE FIRE TRAINING

F L O O R P L A N S :
(page 1 of ___)

Diagram the floor plan on this page for the **BASEMENT.**   Identify which scenarios will be used.

Scenario _____ (see pages ____, ____, ____, & ____).

Continue for all floors of structure.

DEPARTMENT OF FIRE AND RESCUE SERVICES
MONTGOMERY COUNTY, MARYLAND

REQUEST FOR LIVE FIRE TRAINING

SECTION III

-- Responsibilities:

> Instructor in Charge

> Instructors

> Safety Officer(s)

> Support Personnel

-- Students Statement of Training

-- Participant Lists By Department and Corporations

-- Responsibility of OIC- Immediate Pre-Burn Procedure

-- Post Burn Procedure

FIELD SUPPORT SERVICES/SAFETY OFFICE

REQUEST FOR LIVE FIRE TRAINING

RESPONSIBILITIES OF INSTRUCTOR IN CHARGE:
(To be completed prior to start of training exercise)

COMPLETED:

1. PLANNING & COORDINATION OF ALL TRAINING ACTIVITIES:_____

2. ASSIGNED INSTRUCTORS:_____

Attack hose lines (must be from a separate water supply and backup engine)   _____
Functional assignments   _____
Teaching assignments   _____

3. BRIEF INSTRUCTORS ON RESPONSIBILITIES: _____

Accounting for assigned students   _____
Assessing student performance   _____
Protective clothing and breathing apparatus equipment inspection   _____
Monitoring for safe operations   _____
Achieving tactical and training objectives   _____
Review planned scenarios and assignments for each scenario.   _____

4. ASSIGN SUPPORT STAFF AS NEEDED: _____

EMS Unit assigned, and it's location   _____
Communications channels established   _____
Water supply operations   _____
Apparatus and equipment staging   _____
Breathing apparatus and air supply   _____
Rehabilitation area established   _____
Public relations   _____

FIELD SUPPORT SERVICES/SAFETY OFFICE

REQUEST FOR LIVE FIRE TRAINING

RESPONSIBILITIES OF INSTRUCTOR IN CHARGE:
(Continued)

COMPLETED:

5.   Ensure that a Rapid Intervention Team of four individuals (3 firefighters and an officer) are in full protective clothing with backup hoseline ready.   _____

6.   Scenarios are to be based on a sequential burning plan that meets Sections 5-2.9, 5-2.10, and 5-2.11 OF NFPA 1403.   _____

7.   Ensure that no more than nine (9) people (firefighters/officers & instructors) are in the training structure during a burn.   _____

8.   Ensure that all persons in the training area adhere to the standard.   _____

9.   Inspect building integrity prior to each fire.   _____

10.   Monitor all activities to ensure safe practices.   _____

I understand that the above listed items outline my responsibilities, and I have provided for the completion of these responsibilities according to the standard.

_____   _____

Rank/Signature of Instructor in Charge: Date:

Comments: _____

_____

_____

FIELD SUPPORT SERVICES/SAFETY OFFICE

REQUEST FOR LIVE FIRE TRAINING

RESPONSIBILITIES OF THE SAFETY OFFICER:

(To be completed prior to start of the drill)

_____ 1. Review all pre-burn information such as: training scenarios, water supply, and initial and follow-up inspection reports.

_____ 2. Complete an inspection of the structure to be burned, and identify support areas.

_____ 3. Verify that primary and alternate water supplies are being used.

_____ 4. Verify that a Rapid Intervention team has been established.

_____ 5. If additional safety personnel are required, provide appropriate assignments and briefings.

_____ 6. Prevent unsafe acts from occurring by intervention and termination.

_____ 7. Eliminate unsafe conditions.

_____ 8. Ensure compliance by participants and instructors of personal equipment required:

      1. Full protective clothing
      2. Self-contained breathing apparatus
      3. Personal alarm device and pass tag

_____ 9. Coordinate lighting of fires with instructor in charge.

_____ 10. Ensure that no more than nine (9) people are in the structure during a burn.

_____ 11. Ensure that all participants are accounted for, both before and after each evolution.

I understand that the above listed items outline my responsibilities, and I have provided for the completion of each of these, according to the standard.

_____   _____
Rank/Signature of the Safety Officer   _Date_

FIELD SUPPORT SERVICES/SAFETY OFFICE

REQUEST FOR LIVE FIRE TRAINING

Comments:_____

_____

_____

_____

FIELD SUPPORT SERVICES/SAFETY OFFICE

REQUEST FOR LIVE FIRE TRAINING

RESPONSIBILITY OF INSTRUCTOR (S):

(To be completed prior to the start of the drill)

_____ 1. Ensure that you've received the appropriate briefing from the instructor in charge as to your assignment.

_____ 2. Prior to each evolution, inspect the students, determine the appropriate protective clothing, envelope is being used.

_____ 3. Account for your assigned students both before and after each evolution.

_____ 4. Be alert for unsafe or hazardous conditions; initiate action to terminate that problem.

_____ 5. Ensure that effective communications are maintained between you and the instructor in charge.

I understand that the above listed items outline my responsibilities, and I have provided for the completion of these according to the standard.

_____	_____
Rank/Signature of Instructor	*Date*
_____	_____
Rank/Signature of Instructor	*Date*
_____	_____
Rank/Signature of Instructor	*Date*
_____	_____
Rank/Signature of Instructor	*Date*

Comments: _____
_____
_____

FIELD SUPPORT SERVICES/SAFETY OFFICE

REQUEST FOR LIVE FIRE TRAINING

RESPONSIBILITIES OF SUPPORT PERSONNEL:
(To be completed prior to the start of the drill)

_____ 1. Receive briefing from the instructor in charge as to responsibilities in support of this drill.

_____ 2. Ensure that all appropriate equipment required for the completion of my responsibilities is on site and ready for use prior to the start of the drill.

_____ 3. Account for all assigned personnel both before and after each evolution.

_____ 4. Report to the instructor in charge any unsafe or hazardous conditions.

I understand that the above listed items outline my responsibilities, and have provided for the completion of these according to the standard.

_____   _____
Rank/Signature of Support Personnel   *Date*

_____   _____
Rank/Signature of Support Personnel   *Date*

_____   _____
Rank/Signature of Support Personnel   *Date*

_____   _____
Rank/Signature of Support Personnel   *Date*

Comments:

_____

_____

_____

_____

_____

_____

FIELD SUPPORT SERVICES/SAFETY OFFICE

REQUEST FOR LIVE FIRE TRAINING

STUDENT'S STATEMENT OF TRAINING:
(To be completed prior to the drill)

I certify that I have received permission from my fire chief to participate in this drill, and have successfully completed one of the following training requirements.

(NOTE: falsifying this information will be reported to the appropriate fire chief.)

1. Successful completion of the Montgomery County Department of Fire and Rescue Services Essentials of Firefighting.

2. Successful completion of any basic firefighter training course in which the Montgomery County Department of Fire and Rescue Services has granted equivalency.

3. Successful completion of the Montgomery County Department of Fire and Rescue Services career recruit school.

4. Successful completion of all course work associated with the Montgomery County Department of Fire and Rescue Services Essentials of Firefighting, or recruit school, that is using this training drill as part of the training program.

See Signature Pages That Follow

The Remainder of this Page is Blank

FIELD SUPPORT SERVICES/SAFETY OFFICE

REQUEST FOR LIVE FIRE TRAINING

Participant List:

NAME	SIGNATURE	RANK/STATION/SHIFT

FIELD SUPPORT SERVICES/SAFETY OFFICE

REQUEST FOR LIVE FIRE TRAINING

IMMEDIATE PRE-BURN PROCEDURES

RESPONSIBILITY OF THE OFFICER-IN-CHARGE:

_____ 1. Ventilation opening made in the roof, or existing opening covered and ready to open.

_____ 2. Fire sets prepared:

_____ Class A materials only.

_____ No flammable liquids.

_____ No contaminated materials.

_____ Sequential burn plan scenarios established.

_____ All instructors and support staff briefed:

_____ Scenarios provided and reviewed.
_____ Instructor and staff walk-through of the burn area.
_____ Instructor and support staff assignments made.
_____ Safety Officer assignment noted.
_____ Command vest used for key staff, safety and support personnel.

_____ 3. All participants briefed:

_____ Floor plans reviewed
_____ Building interior walk-through
_____ Introduction of instructors, support and safety staff along with assignments
_____ Safety roles
_____ Building evacuation procedures
_____ Evacuation signal (demonstrate)

_____ 4. Water supply:

_____ Primary water supply established
_____ Secondary/Alternate water supply assigned or established

FIELD SUPPORT SERVICES/SAFETY OFFICE

REQUEST FOR LIVE FIRE TRAINING

IMMEDIATE PRE-BURN PROCEDURES

RESPONSIBILITY OF THE OFFICER-IN-CHARGE *(page 2):*

_____ 5. All hose lines checked:

_____ Sufficient size for the area of the fire involvement.
_____ Charged and test flowed.
_____ Instructors assigned to each line.
_____ Adequate number of personnel.

_____ 6. Necessary tools and equipment positioned.

_____ 7. Participants checked:

_____ Approved for protective clothing.
_____ Self-contained breathing apparatus.
_____ Adequate SCBA air supplies (spare cylinders, and/or cascade system).
_____ All equipment properly donned.
_____ PATs collected by the accountability officer.

_____ 8. *Command post established.*

_____ 9. All apparatus in position.

_____10. Rapid response team identified and in position.

_____11. All hose lines (attack and backup) in position.

_____12. Emergency escape routes properly identified.

_____13. Location of emergency evacuation assembly area identified.

_____14. Location of entry and exit routes for emergency vehicles.

_____15. BLS unit on location.

_____16. Rehabilitation area established.

FIELD SUPPORT SERVICES/SAFETY OFFICE

REQUEST FOR LIVE FIRE TRAINING

IMMEDIATE PRE-BURN PROCEDURES

RESPONSIBILITY OF THE OFFICER-IN-CHARGE *(page 3):*

_____17. Fire flow calculations completed and apparatus/hoselines meet requirements for offensive operations.

_____18. Weather reports obtained.

_____19. Parking areas designated and marked.

_____20. Apparatus staging area assigned.

_____21. Liaison established, if applicable, to work with outside agencies.

_____22. Operations area (hot zone) established and marked.

_____23. Communications frequencies established, and equipment obtained and assigned.

I certify that I have provided for the above listed items prior to the burning:

_____   _____
Rank/Signature of Instructor in Charge   *Date*

Comments:

_____
_____
_____
_____
_____
_____

FIELD SUPPORT SERVICES/SAFETY OFFICE

REQUEST FOR LIVE FIRE TRAINING

POST BURN PROCEDURES

RESPONSIBILITIES OF THE INSTRUCTOR-IN-CHARGE:

The Instructors in charge is to ensure that post-burn procedures are completed following <u>each</u> live-fire evolution in a structure.

_____   1.   All personnel are accounted for.

_____   2.   Fire area is overhauled as required.

_____   3.   The building has been inspected for hazards if additional training is to follow.

_____   4.   Training critique conducted.

_____   5.   Documentation of unusual conditions or events.

_____   6.   Injuries incurred and treatment rendered.

_____   7.   If injuries or accidents occurred - appropriate First Report of Injuries, Liability statements, SIIR reports, witness statements and narrative reports provided.

Upon completion of the final burn, ensure that all appropriate documents required for this live fire training evolution and any supplemental reports are attached to this document and returned to the safety office, Station 20.

_____   _____

Rank/Signature of Instructor in Charge   *Date*